WORDS IN ADHD

Keyuana Rosemond

ISBN: 978-0-9863813-4-8

BM Webster Publishing, LLC.

For more information about scheduling the author for speaking engagements, or book discounts please contact the author at the email address provided:

keyuanasrose@gmail.com

Connect with the author on social media for updates and event information.

Facebook: Keyuana TooShort Rosemond
Instagram: rhoyalmastermind

This book is dedicated to everyone that has loved, lost and dared to live. Special thanks to my tribe that made this possible and my God who created the will.

To those that have a voice...and those that feel like they don't...this is for U.

Table of Contents

Dream Sequence

Heartless, all because you left me

Had an opportunity to have a love I've never seen,

Thoughts of loving only you and building a home
meant for 2,

You're the only thing I see, when you're far I want you
desperately,

Trying to find the words to say,

Thinking of my love today,

Wishing she would be right here to have and hold me
near and dear,

To her heart.

And I'd promise we would never part,

Enjoying constant ecstasy,

Cuz with you love I'd be so FREE.

Free from all the bull and games,

promise I'll hold all your pain and pump it all right
through my veins,

letting it

Travel up and down my streams, knowing I'd fulfill
your dreams

With nothing else but only me

turning

Nightmares into fantasies cuz we're alone when you're asleep and I hear you yearning desperately wanting all the pain to go, missing me I want you so

Even though you closed your eyes,

You open up and then surprise

You see

Me laying here right next to you, always here to comfort you, free like birds so fly we flew...

Holding you tightly as we,

as we,

submerge into one entity,

Releasing energy, causing an emotional crash as we,

as we,

Illuminate the light of our love as your river flows strong and fast, shimmering on my tongue and lips and just like that my pain's eclipsed by the current of your ever flowing love and undying passion.

You see you know these things about me that no one ever could,

You are the perfect ending to a scary movie, the

epilogue to a literary masterpiece.

The light to my darkest days and the sky to my constellation,

Woman,

You are so tangible to me, so much so that you elude me,

I just want you near, so please reveal yourself, tired of playing hide and go get it,

So come get me, I'm here waiting for your love to appear

And when it comes I promise your arrival won't be in vain

Woman I just want to keep you,

Hold you hostage with my desire and wrap you up in a cocoon of bliss nurtured with ecstasy and topped off with the sweetest kiss.

Gazing into your soft brown eyes I see you,

Your essence, your beauty

You reveal your soul to me with every stare and I return the gaze.

Connecting with you at every level known to man,

Discovering the nature of your heart and the origin of your love,

You intrigue me to no end and frequently I find

myself caught up in the rapture of your embrace.

I've found something wonderful and I can't let go

I want to keep you in my treasure chest and preserve all your goodness

I want to bronze your love and put you on my trophy shelf

So when people come around

I can show you off proudly

Claiming you as the prize you are and letting the world know how proud I am to be yours.

I want to bottle up your love and sell it to whomever will buy, proclaiming it as the best stuff on earth, Snapple ain't got shit on this!!

I want to do all these things and more for you and for us

All because ...I love you

And now... I'm standing here at this crossroad, knowing that it was you the one who I belong to, the one who has my heart tattoo

I envision being in your arms for eternity

You,

Loving me,

Giving me that serenity,

That comfort, that calm sensation of security and companionship

Searching for myself and finding you in my identity, tells me that I belong with you and no one else,

Sure others try and I attempt but at the end of the day,

It's you I see as they walk away from me, leaving.

Exiting just as swiftly as they came,

But your existence is ever present,

Unchanging

It fills me with joy to the degree of zenith,

Second to none, first to everything

Take me love,

I've been waiting for your loving embrace forever

And now that you're here I just want to hold you,

keep you

Near me, strengthening our love day by day

Fighting and surviving, like the last one on the island or the fittest man conquering everything in his path,

I belong with you, to you,

True you,

say that its destiny that we met the way we did

And I'll stop denying that I was fighting my feelings

from day one

And each moment my love grows and evolves into something indescribable, Unexplainable, unimaginable.

So amazing it is to have found you.

Your blueprint is mine and as you write your name I see me

In your heart and on your mind,

Now I'm not a mind reader or a fortune teller but I can see my future in your eyes, in my palm.

On your left hand.

Cast your fears aside and trust in me, just once more,

I belong with you and no one else.

And as long as words flow from my lips,

I'll profess my love for you in speech, in song, in ink

You're the only other half that makes me whole

I belong to you because it's in my pedigree that I was born to love you,

So let me fulfill my destiny and carry out my duty to you

My love,

I belong with you and no one else.

R.I.P

My heart is still intact but 2 arteries have snapped,

Ceasing circulation but the blood flows through my ink,

Air trapped in my lungs, stomach contorts and twists

Cuz my feelings of pure bliss have exploded and been purported into resentment and longing for your love to reappear,

Hating to disappear from this world we created where you authored our book and I illustrated our story through photographs and memories, sweet kisses, and I love you's were our thing and the resonation of your name on my heart remains.

What's wrong now?

And again you need your space so now it's build up and destroy, create and dissolve, this cycle you induce when you think of only you....and apparently there's no 'us" since the "s" that stands for security and sincerity has vanished....

Her words single handedly intended to free her imprisonment so she proceeded to rip into my whole existence, rip into my personality,

R.I.P my whole world apart in one instant

With every word my heart continues to rip, tear, and

singe till nothing remains;

No story, no "us",

Just u.

Because I fell in love with you...

Nothing else mattered,

Not the weather,

Not work,

Not even those high ass gas prices,

Making,

Trips to the "Chi" at $4.25 a gallon for a day,

Riding the "L" and sipping on Baba's Lemonade,

The thanksgivings and New Year's celebrations,

See nothing mattered except you and our time duration

We would sneak off for rendezvous before we even became 1,

15B or Winter 212 were our locations,

Crutches couldn't even stop me from reaching your destination

Because I fell in love with you...

Daydream (SOC)

Colors swirling all around me,

Pink, green...I lay on the freshly pressed sheets anticipating, waiting, longing for you to draw near. I inhale the sweet aroma of your signature scent and it excites me.. .Entices me...Cueing images of your silhouette approaching me caressing my body with lips and kissing me to ecstasy... Elevating my senses and awakening my heart with this electrifying passion and love overflowing... you have restored my desire to love again and for that I am indebted to you. I graciously thank you for rekindling this fire within me that was once doused... I applaud you for not only being patient, but for loving me accidentally yet honestly while still being the wonderful friend you are and remaining supportive in all my endeavors.. As I lay on these sheets, I dream of you comforting me and needing me as desperately as I need you... and no matter where our future lies, my heart holds a place for you and is awaiting the day when your soul will fill it.

"I want to go to Philly with you" she said

On this journey of self - discovery she wants to accompany....me

The driver and her the passenger on this foggy road with no clear direction or path that's been laid.

Still traveling, her and me,

Knowing not where we are or,

our destination but venturing nonetheless on this possible road to redemption and preservation with no map or compass, using only the directions of our hearts.

I admit,

it used to be enough to be with her, compromising everything just to make us work.

Now,

it feels like she's a million miles away.

Drifting upstream while I'm swimming furiously against a riptide current tryna save her

to bring her back to me.

Sometimes I fear

that maybe it was I who pushed her away,

made her life stressful and

even though we could waste time with the blame game,

I just want to cherish our time together.

When she's married with kids,

I don't ever want her to forget about her honeydew

The best boyfriend she never had,

I love her and no matter what

I never want her to forget that

or me.

All because she loved me....

I took her to monumental heights on a magic carpet ride we flew,

Soared above the clouds and became tourists snapping photos and scrapbooking our lives together, syncing the memories with the fantasies, accepting an alternate reality of pure bliss.

Rejecting the feelings of insecurity, neglecting tenderness and kind words, ignoring this eminent absence of love.

You see,

she loved me with her highest hopes.

I was her Prince Charming but I'm not being modest honestly

I was content being her present.

She wanted forever,

and with those four letters she attempted to arrest my soul and handcuff my heart.

But

instead I decided

that prison was for pussies and I devised an elaborate scheme to get in between all the while duplicating the keys not needing to break free but just leave and walk out when I'm ready...and I did.

Repeatedly

running from love, hiding from commitment, evading the thing that is monogamy and probably had more girls than Maxim magazine.

And yet

I'm here

Trying to undo the wrongs I did to all of them.

Trying to be the best that I can be, in this world of fantasy, defined by feelings and emotions, ignoring all my selfish notions of escape.

You see,

I'm trying hard to be better and with you girl I think I can

like that little engine train,

chugging,

making attempts to,

breathe you,

from my own element of love.

God sent me his angel ordained from above.

Wrap me with your wings Queen,

embrace me,

love me,

I know I don't deserve it

but

I promise I'd be worth it.

Addicted

I'm in my straight jacket, staring at these walls, going through withdraws in my draws cuz I miss u,

Give me 10 ccs of that methadone stat,

Addicted to your love girl I swear that it's crack,

Your potion is hypnotic and so damn toxic, I lock lips and take sips of the serum, as it finds its way down my throat and through my body it releases energy and sends a message to synapses and snaps my body into action tackling your massive personality and pummeling your body into submission with my love.

As I'm,

sending

chills down through your spine inducing convulsions with the motion of my muscle on your pearl,

and as you

reach that peak of ecstasy thanking God and newly finding religion, I stop and repeat the cycle 'til your faucet runs hot and starts squirting outta control leaving your love on lips and my heart on your kiss, just think, your lady and my face until it's pink, I would bottle up your love and it would be my favorite drink. I'd call it desire, more potent than cocaine, stronger than the chronic, it is my narcotic leaving me inebriated and intoxicated at just one ounce of you....and as I speak I'm going through withdraws got me scratching, itching, and fienin' for another hit bound to this bed, staring at these walls going through withdraws in my draws cuz I miss you.

Wedding Vows part 2

With this ring I be wed, damn never thought I'd be here throwin' in the towel and holding your hand at the altar. Standing scared yet proudly at your side awaiting our fate, to have and to hold, jumping out the window, goin' half on a son vacationing in Rio. I see myself in your eyes and you in mine and as they sparkle and shine, I see the gleam. So peaceful and serene. As long as we both shall live, together as one... and yes it won't all be fun, there will be some trials and tribulations, but with our love ma we'll make it. Outlasting all our troubles and building a foundation so solid, no man can break it.. .This I will do for you and this I will do for us, I offer my sincerest abilities of love, respect, intelligence, patience, and kindness, gathering all your sorrows, pain and uncertainties on my back to carry you through our trying times. I will protect you, provide for you and cherish you. For as long as I live and as long as God graces this Earth with your presence. I love you.

Untitled II

{Pressure, decisions, all these inquisitions of responsibility and fate,

I scream but no one listens,

I shout and act out but everyone turns the other cheek.}.

Don't know if you think they're pretty, but my wings have been clipped,

From the point of origin to the feather,

Trying to weather this hurricane typhoon-esque state,

Tears and emotions flowing, rushing in a riptide of depression, self-blame and loathing,

Trying to make sense of dollars and organize my thoughts,

Searching deep within for inner peace,

Clarity,

Trying to restore my sanity but these nightmares keep haunting me,

I'm having

Tremors at twilight cuz my body is at rest but my mind never sleeps,

And finally its constant activity is draining me, screaming, shouting, and crying out for help.

The constant pain and uncertainties within are affecting my stability and causing insanity.

I feel as though I am a modern day VanGogh with the paper as my canvas and the pen as my brush. Capturing my story and my innermost feelings, becoming one with my psychotic tendencies as no one will hear me but me.

Blasting Day & Night on repeat thinking Kid Cudi dedicated his lament to me.

Seeking this thing called clarity, blowing to Frankie Beverly and Maze, in a daze, letting that Purple Haze lift me, and take me away from my problems,

providing an escape from my situations cuz situationally,

I am the center of drama and everyone but me is the center of my life.

This imbalance is fuckin' with the psychosis my drug induces to put me in a cool state,

Shaking uncontrollably,

realizing that I'm crying,

all because I'm trying to please everyone but me.

Thinking of their happiness before my own not realizing that happiness itself is foreign to me,

Trying to recollect the last moment in time that my mind was at equilibrium, resting, balanced,

stable.

Able to recollect and recall my downfall, from grace and place the blame on a face in another space and time, but the only reflection I find is mine.

Protector, provider, I observed these roles historically reserved for man played out by my mother, Protector, provider, caregiver, disciplinarian, parent,

You see,

it was her there 24-7 while you picked and chose when you were going to participate or rather facilitate my development cuz you damn sure didn't contribute, didn't teach, didn't mold me

taught no lessons, showed no love.

I sat reminiscing on my childhood, reflecting on the impact of your absence, realizing that your truancy is indeed what shaped me.

Protector, provider, these roles reserved for man I equate with me, so I believe that it is my duty, to do all the things for my wife and family that you didn't, anticipating the day when the titles wife and mother are attached to my name, pledging my allegiance to my seeds and my responsibilities,

you see nothing is more important than family, well at least it is to me but I guess we don't agree.

But I digress

and suggest

that you take lessons from my mother and even from

your daughter on how to be a good man, good husband, good father, and maybe you'll finally realize that yeah you fucked up.

Ages 13 to 17, single parent home, momma laid off, too young to get a job, so I had to hit the block,

to make up for the shit you ain't provide, with my glock on my thigh, hat cocked to the side,

Forced to grow up way too soon,

Missing out little things like barbeques with the crew or hangin' out on the stoop,

But instead I pretended to be you, making money, paying bills, and providing for the home,

Leavin' moms all alone to deal with me, lyin' about my income and running the streets,

I was the monster you created, when somehow you dissipated and ignored this family unit you created, only to uproot and begin another in a different location,

with a different cast.

And I would be fakin' if I said I didn't miss you then,

And I can't pretend it still doesn't affect me, but presently your absence is required not requested,

because without you I'm still blessed and

I've forgiven but I'm never forgettin',

To protect and provide cuz u were missin'

If I Must Die (21)

21 years is a blessing that many I know don't see,

And sometimes I'm even astonished that I could get here,

In middle school we predicted and planned our funerals but couldn't see life

We authored wills and testaments,

And now I'm here still alive.

But

If I must die

Let it not be like my brother Josh who didn't have a chance or Zack who didn't have a choice.

If I must die let it be nobly on the battlefield of love or in the arena of righteousness,

Within the walls of academia and purpose I will rest,

Tomb filled with the works of scholars like Carter G. Woodson and Audre Lorde

If I must die, let it be in a world where sexism, racism, and homophobia don't matter,

Because they are non-existent,

If I must die, let it be in the arms of my soul mate,

I'm talkin' bout

goin' out notebook style, like I die, you die, we die together type soul mates,

If I must die, let me go in peace so I can meet you and feel your warm embrace comfort me,

If I must die let it not be in the season where roses bloom,

With people singing "gone too soon" cuz here lies an angel,

If I must go I'll go, but only to be with him so I can sit at the table and mix and mingle with John, Paul, finally meet Aaliyah, watch Mikey moonwalk live, and kick knowledge with 'Pac,

Death is inevitable, but when I go, I hope everyone remembers to laugh and smile for the memories and not cry at the funeral.

For you Grandad

Inconceivable...

You used to listen to Donny Hathaway and Gil Scott Heron talk about the ghetto and revolutions,

While Roberta was killing me softly, little did I know that she wasn't the only one killing you.

Born in (1914) in the heyday of the Ku Klux Klan, you were built to last as the only thing that put fear in your heart was losing your family,

And you wished a motherfucker would threaten them, this no nonsense attitude was passed down through the generations of black panthers and civil rights soldiers I'm proud to call my family,

I recall helping clean out my grandma's closet and finding buttons from your city council campaign,

that you won.

Winner, champion, that's what you stood for and that's what you are,

So I guess that's why I was so distraught when they said you had a stroke, dementia, a couple months to live.

It seemed like all the fight within you vanished and the facts of life were overwhelming and dictating your fate, which up 'til now you were always the master of.

You used to tell us stories about your life, intriguing me with your strength and perseverance cuz I don't know if I would have been able to live in a time where blacks were blatantly oppressed and even though our oppression is structural and covert now, I admire the courage of you and Nana, holding the family together through various trials and tribulations...no question, not a chore, but a duty and a priority.

You are the type of man any girl would dream to have, and the qualities that you possess were given to my mother through your son,

And if I could be half the woman she is, I'd proudly proclaim my lineage to the Blackfoot and Cherokee tribes in your blood line cuz I get annoyed when folks talk about having Indian in them and there's no question that you have tribal ties,

But your reflection is self-defined by one word

Black.

You see, you were the one that instilled Black Pride into all of us and as I stare at my reflection, I am proud to say that I wouldn't have it any other way,

My skin and my roots are a reflection of yours,

Strong, tribal, and indigenous to this nation no matter how much discrimination you endured at the hands of others...

Granddad, it's your green girl and if you hear me, I want you to know that I appreciate you.

Your caring spirit lives on through us and the love of knowledge you expressed lives on through me,

As long as I live, my pen will bleed the blood of your passion for scholarship and justice,

So sleep old man, rest cuz it's long overdue,

You've been fighting death way too long

I guess now's your time to surrender.

Identity Pt. I

I am a minority,

Black GLBT who just happens to be a woman,

And with all this legislation the government is debating, it seems like my identity is on trial,

The system is designed for them, and my destiny is failure by their design, in this nation.

Bruised and abused, giving up is my resignation,

And if I resign, I'll sign my name on the dotted line accepting this,

But until the last breath is sighed, and the accumulation of every tear I cried matters not,

I will fight.

Every struggle,

Every altercation I'm facing is draining leaving me wasted,

Energy seeps out the pores of my flesh,

Shocking me to the core of my existence,

But still

I am pushing, pulling, acting against the seemingly immovable force that is ignorance,

You ignorant few, attempt to, box me up into your, categorical domains of chains, individuality ignored you see me as a sinner.

Another one destined to enter the floodgates of hell,

Dwelling in the darkness crying, begging me to change my ways, at an early age trapped inside a gilded cage, torn between acceptance and accepting me.

Now I don't wanna go on a tangent, shouting, screaming, wanting revolution, tryna find a solution, to reverse this mind polluting,

Fueling the brutality toward homosexuality, beatings and bashings in the name of religion,

While the government turns its cheek like the Old Testament,

Instead of just arresting them,

While my boy on the block gets 5 years for possession?

This is democracy at its finest,

Red, white, and blue is for you,

Only if you meet the requirements,

Ethnicity no scratch that, race, class, and sexuality,

And in reality we live in a country that teaches hate, failing to appreciate the mosaic that created the fabric of this nation,

Embracing exclusion and discrimination, while

masking it with apple pies and smiles,

Falsely advertising acceptance, you display this façade
while purposely planting images of the black
experience and gay life,

conveying messages stereotyping my life.

It's hard to make a good first impression when
American society has formed its perception of me.

Before a word is spoken, my entire being is broken
down into,

Categorical domains of chains, individuality ignored,
you see me as a sinner

But I know that Jesus loves me so I still feel like a
winner.

We just wanna live like you,

Free from hostility or the possibility of being slain for
just breathing,

We are humans too,

We cry,

We bleed,

We laugh,

We love,

So please

Just let us LIVE.

My Immortal Beloved

My Immortal Beloved,

There's so much that time cannot erase.

Tears splattering, glass shattering,

Breaking the silence with a sonic boom that permeates all barriers of uncertainties, sleeping loudly to your lullaby while my moonlight sonata plays as our score,

Dark and menacing,

In Philadelphia we soared to new heights,

Breaking barriers and laying foundations,

Now my,

beloved is drifting into the abyss and the fires of our legacy are doused,

Drowning the passion and serenity that existed,

Into a black hole of existing,

Only in our memories.

Carnations used to bear the sweet scent of devotion,

Now they carry a stench of regret and sorrow,

Once pure,

Fresh as the first winter snow,

Our love,

Transcended boundaries of tradition,

It stood alone to fight for us,

Unknowing contenders in the contest of fate,

Our union: a partnership of souls aligning with similar passions and ambitions, weaving a tapestry that illustrated our life,

Exhibiting courage and defining love,

Defying all odds,

Strengthening our bond,

Admiration: only an understatement cuz truly I exalted thee,

Like the queen you are destined to be,

A throne was built for all to see,

With a foundation of trust and honesty,

Immortal Beloved.

Our portrait, once upon a time that was envied by all, is tarnished

Tattered ruins of a love undone,

Became a destructive vortex,

Devouring all who encountered it,

Our flowers, once full of life, are charred roses

Singed by the flames of resentment and pain,

Petals ashen and in desperate need of hydration ... My Immortal Beloved,

Is slowly dying in the darkness where I dwell,

Masking hurt with vengeance,

Attempting to heal the wounds of heartbreak,

While I stitch and repair my heart from aching.

Souls trying to reconnect and become the life support that brings Ying and yang back,

Resuscitating, reviving the bond that held us intact

My Immortal Beloved

Her spirit surrounds me even when she's gone,

Flying deftly she soars.

We're exploring free.

Yet I still long for her CAPTIVITY.

If I Were a Writer

If I were a writer,

I'd design a lyrical monologue for the vagina,

Kinda like the syllables in words, curbing the appetite for verbs,

Arousing the passion for nouns and sounds,

Incredible soliloquies with similes abound,

If I were a writer,

I'd be a fighter for revolution,

Crafting solutions to the problematic actions of problem addicts,

Raping, killing, robbing citizens of hopes and dreams,

Not talking fiends, but referencing the government and their disposition, Lack of intervention in issues of poverty and breaking Anglo tradition,

If I were a writer,

I'd scribe a message to the youth of America,

Imploring them to have hope for their future,

Cuz the structure of our institutions exude apathy,

Causing proverbial bullets of sexism, discrimination,

and racism to clap back at the 10% of those who try,

90% don't care,

Lacking empathy causing death and destruction to themselves,

Frustrated with a system that supplies more drugs than books,

More diseases than classes,

And more guns than competent teachers,

If I were a writer,

I'd illustrate the struggles of my people,

In a petition to Congress declaring our issues aggressively

Cuz we're sick and tired

Of being tired and sick,

Unable to afford doctor visits but able to buy 40's and Newports

Structural genocide alive in urban areas,

With more visible liquor stores than schools,

Generationally creating fools,

Education amiss along with adequate public service,

If I were a writer,

I'd express my frustrations to anyone who could read,

My passion for uplift and peace super cedes prejudice,

Fighting the battle,

Predicating truth,

Bleeding for belief in a people overcoming a system,

But I'm not a writer,

Just a fighter, an advocate,

A spirit of truth that needs life to survive,

But my community is dying,

How can I stay alive?

I want to

Relive you - even though the pain seemed hard to bear at times,

Revisiting our love with a new perspective to

Revitalize our passion, desire, and excitement for each other,

Refreshing the possibility of our love, Re-Incarnating the spirit that created the initial spark that

Revealed our yearning for the enchantment that love brings.

I want to release the feelings of resentment toward you. Realize that we both made mistakes in this. No one is perfect but we can Recreate our story, Re-illustrating our chapters and Revamping the expectations that we hold for one another. Rebuilding us is the ultimate goal,

Recanting all the insults, Repressing our Regret, and giving Reconsideration to the Rebirth of our union.

Reconciling

Rekindling

Reconnecting with U

Addiction Pt.1

Ur my addiction,

Fix,

Kiss like Cocaine,

Heroin,

Ur my Chocolate High,

One hit of you sends chills down my spine as I roll my eyes to the back of my mind,

Trembling, Shaking,

Still going thru withdraws but in another place,

My heart is beating from a million miles away

But your voice on the phone keeps me from going pure insane,

Blowed off your love,

Intoxicated off your passion,

Veins flowing with devotion off the motion of your presence in my heart,

as it pumps it completes every sentence,

In a message to my brain,

That makes a passage to my heart,

We're apart and I'm shaking,

My insides are aching,

Taking small breaths to stop from hyperventilating,

To keep from suffocating,

From your love,

Or the absence of it,

I'm dying from afar,

I think I need some methadone,

'til I get home,

Then I can make you moan,

But for now I'm still alone.

Purpose? SOC

I want something to live for like air to oxygen, word to page, breath to life, worth dying, something that will make or break, no need to fake cuz I got love for, passion in my body for this thing that makes my heart beat, giving energy to my feet as they become the vessel of direction, directing the journey like the captain to the ship, and I'm starboard sailing, speeding toward my destiny, head first I'll dive in, and if my ship capsizes before I reach the port, I'll abide then, knowing that I attempted to steer clear of the storm. I need something to fuel me, bejewel me out of the constant lull of reality, sketching labyrinths of adventure, never-ending, each voyage a mission for success, adeptly setting out to solve the mysteries, collecting clues to achieve the solution leading to freedom, then re-entering the maze to foster new thinking, forging pathways of perseverance and determination. I need that thing to keep me focused, so I can see my name on a poster, so I can do it for my culture, showing that a misunderstood child of the burbs, that liked to speak English, teased cuz she couldn't decipher Ebonics, chronically criticized for acting "white" can do it then that youngin' in Southfield can also succeed in America.. .I need that, I want that, I live for the opportunity to have that...I need something to live for, give for, cry for, lie for, try for, die for... I need that something.

Pulsing, pulsating, punishing, pulmonary beats,

This day, a day of love, a day of showing sweet sentiments of emotion,

Pulsing, heart races as you hear a faint buzz,

Into the distance you know what that un-mistakable sound is,

He's summoning her again,

Pulsating, messages sending action to synapses as they take in the images,

Attracting the eyes of the room, projecting your emotions across the room,

The discomfort you feel as he enters,

And then,

All the energy races to your mind,

And through your body, replaying scene after scene of how this would go but in reality,

You never thought that it would be like this,

Every dream, illusions and rose colored fantasies,

Imagining that one day you two could be, as you are,

Like you are in another place.

Punishing,

The moments,

Those moments when he's welcomed by everyone,

And the colors start to show, primary and true, only you realize there's only 3 hues not 6,

6 the number of the proud, fighters in their own game,

Constant players in the round you are playing,

Now she speaks words so brief yet tender,

Joy and laughter fill the air,

All is well again,

And you,

This intruder into the perfect paradise, are a bystander.

An outside observer in this snow globe like fantasyland

Where all is acknowledged except your eminent suicide, slowly dying internally,

The words that flowed from her lips were the dagger,

The last blow to bring you to your knees,

"He's her boyfriend"

This phrase though innocent in manner, sends your body into shock and sheer emotional distress, everyone smiles with approving eyes,

And at that moment, you realize that you're nothing more than a friend to them, and that is all you'll ever

Be.

Just 12 hours ago, it was you holding her,

Comforting her in your arms,

She was yours,

You were cheering and taping her shows,

She whispered "I love you" in that soft sweet tone,

Aspartame filled kisses, saccharin sweetened promises,

You vowed to be there for her as long as she'll have you,

But In that moment he became heroic, though it is you who shields her from the dark,

And every second, the dagger is plunged deeper and deeper into your heart,

You're nothing.

Her silence confirms it.

You're shrinking now,

Becoming smaller and shorter,

Reducing yourself to this secret,

To a lie,

Forcing a single tear to drop,

And descend,

From your silent eyes.

A Reflection on Stone Butch Blues

Am I supposed to feel like Pecola, on a rollercoaster of emotion, peering into the shadows?

Sneering at my reflection with repulsion? Moping, hoping that one day they'll truly know what it means for me "to be gendered me", and really accept it,

Really, like I accept it, except for those instances where I endure questions regarding my attire,

Stares of contempt sparking blazing fires, in my soul from their eyes,

Young children begging the question of whether or not I belong in the restroom,

As if I'm not standing there? Participating in reoccurring conversations about my gender, like really that whole "If I wanted a man I would be with one" thing.

Why can't my expression of me be butch but a form of femininity? If I'm sensitive, I'm told to man up.

If I'm strong I'm told to be ladylike. I don't wanna be ladylike but I like ladies and these two aren't the same unless I play a game of wearing a mask and displaying a persona that's homo-nonexistent, dressing like a vixen, emulating "normal" women?

Nope.

Unlike Toni Morrison's character Pecola, I go against my culture, trying to Breedlove from within to the external knowing that the love I have for me is eternal.

Am I supposed to wear femininity as a badge of honor, like Carrol O' Conner in the Heat of the Night, Policing every move, correcting actions, to arrest my character, and interrogate my identity?

Am I supposed to comply quietly, admitting guilt and defecting to reduce my sentence?

Nope.

I stand proudly wrists contorted, adorning stainless steel bracelets, waiting for the day when they can see my face as, a mosaic of the women who were raped and beaten, for wearing BVD'S, DB'S and dildos, still those warriors were standing proud, facing the law, only to receive black eyes and clubs to the skull, blood spilling out their minds, still standing strong with their eyes on the prize.

Am I supposed to be ashamed?

As I take the reins, flooded with emotion, prompted to stare at my reflection with repulsion?

Nah, IM HERE IM QUEER DEAL WITH IT....PERIOD.

The Future

You're DIFFERENT,

You don't speak with a "lagger" tongue,

Illegible Mick Jagger tongue,

That Imma jack your swagger mon,

That "I don't understand you son?"

Look

The word is library,

Not "Liberry",

And it's really kinda scary how niggaz vocabulary, is scarce,

Almost like syntax is ancient history,

Dictionaries so yesterday,

Cuz yesterday they used to find treasures and secrets,

Encrypted in the pages,

Of the books of life,

Textually analyzing,

And conceptualizing their struggles for worldwide consumption, but somehow education became blasé' and intelligence suddenly became uncool,

Undesired, scrutinized

YOU,

Scholars who devote your lives to discovering artifacts,

Deploy strategies to empower the people,

Only to be dejected,

Shamed for being able to recognize names of anything,

Playing "hands up to 85", and NEVER losing,

Assigning categories never-ending to entities of empiricism, and cynicism ensues when you're reading,

Dirty looks

And ostracizing

Cuz you're always theorizing,

And your constant criticizing is equivocated to HATER-ATION,

Cuz proliferation of education, is the greatest challenge you're facing,

In order to UPLIFT,

In hopes to MOTIVATE,

In efforts to save our BLACK NATION.

I AM NOT Grand Valley

You ask me why I don't wear my shirt, my I am Grand Valley shirt?

Well the answer is not intricate, intrinsic or even complicated,

I am NOT Grand Valley.

Let me explain: I am not the conservative, West Michigan principled,

Silver spoon born, corn fed, farm raised, privileged,

Whitewash mono-cultured, "like Oh my God is like Latino Student Union like for Mexicans,

Like the "Blackout" like sounds cool but like do you like have to be black to like go?" mentality,

Black Rose said they stringing up us and I'm tryna loosen my noose,

I am not a token,

Black, gay, woman, who is smart and ambitious and shock ensues... wait there's more,

I can formulate sentences, and though my perspective is unique, stop labeling it "black",

Cuz when someone asks me what I think about racism, poverty, or anything associated with "black stereotypes", I break into hysterics cuz my perspective is not all inclusive, it's MINE.

I am not contagious I swear,

My differences will not rub off on you, so on the Rapid just sit down, listen to your IPod and zone out like the rest of us,

See its things like this that remind me every day that I am not Grand Valley,

To the Provosts I'm just an aspect of a 13 percent population that is categorized into a box "labeled" diversity,

Only to make the Wonder bread have some variety,

Entirely viewed as joke, but I'm not a game see,

This education is valued although I am not,

But I am an individual adding my ideas to the pot, diverse in intellect not just my skin, or my culture.

I am a student, hungry for knowledge, ravishing essays and authors, devouring all the words my appetite can hold,

I am first generation, educated legacy,

I am Detroit, Southfield, Chicago, Grand Rapids,

Oakland, Mexico, San Juan, and Haiti,

Sudan, Nigeria, Bosnia, and New Orleans,

I am the future,

Uniquely an individual,

NOT Grand Valley.

Altruist Intentions?

Don't paint my walls and call it community service,

Don't build a fence and call it charity work,

Philanthropy and advocacy?

Yeah right, advocating looking good posing for a check see,

I refuse to beg for your time or positive attention, but you wanna catch a fit cuz I ask for a commitment? Or continuous investment? No. I refuse to abide this time.

So take your volunteers back on that bus and go on back where you came from,

With your matching hoodies, acting like your two hours will erase all my pain,

Only to go back to your realities where you forget about me see,

You think you know what I need but you have no idea.

There are children dying on my streets without homes, food, or clothes,

I house citizens that have watched their vibrant hopes, pillage their hearts and elope with their colorful dreams, you say you want to serve me? So ask what I need done.

You think you really know what's best for me? Well ask yourself while you sip your hot cocoa in cashmere robes, when's the last time you've seen homes and businesses burned because of prejudice, Folks frozen outta homes, and pushed into tenements,

A family homeless cuz the parents lost their jobs to downsizing,

A 12 year old selling her body to make her own momma a profit,

I bet the tears you've cried in your eyes can't match the heartbreak of a ghetto child's life,

Yet you call me hood, and label me a project implying false progress see,

Work needs to be done that's not mowing my lawns, there hasn't been grass for 20 years.

Stop bringing buses of folks to sweep my streets, all smiles ignoring the blood between their feet,

If you wanna serve me, communication is key, better schools, more attention less negative publicity,

And stop building highways through me,

Walls to by-pass me,

Only to ignore me, acting like I don't exist, like I'm eyesore in the view from your office,

I'm tired of being lied to and beaten, raped and exploited,

My stains run so deep that no bleach can ever cleanse 'em,

If you really wanna help me,

Spend some time and discover what will actually have a purpose,

Don't paint my walls or build a fence and call THAT bullshit community service.

Ode to Miss Lucy

U were never meant to be a hero, but ur cape beat in the wind, beneath ur wings was ur granddaughter, my love, u left, away so quickly but ur spirit she embodies, and our love a test of time and tribulations, I love my love who loved u ever so dearly, now I thank u for giving her to me see, u cared enough to shield her in ur armor and knight her with ur majesty, on her throne she now sits as a princess groomed to

be a queen by ur splendor, and u, watching over her guiding her path and keeping her light shining, today is her 21st birthday, that's 21 years of heartache, 20 of turmoil, 19 perseverance's, 18 strengths, 17 struggles, 16 times she lost count of the heartbreaks, 15 questions she asked God, of 14 tests, 13 triumphs, 12 visions, 11 consultations, 10 real friends, 9 I love you's, 8 disappointments, 7 confrontations, 6 memories, 5 faves, 4 funerals, 3 roomies, 2 lives, 1 love. U were never meant to be a hero but her spirit embodies u, so it's only right for me to thank u for giving me the person that u saved 21 years ago.

B-Boy

You're beautiful,

Crafting sonnets with ur limbs,

Over-extending calves and pirouettes,

Your beautiful,

Soul meets passion,

Making a humble abode in your heart with every leap,

You seek to soar with Icarus,

In flight, your wings sustain the wind,

You soar to monumental elevations,

You're a b-boy, creating beats so soulful that they resurrect the Duke and restore Ray's sight,

Your feet breathe life into post-modernist compositions,

Positions,

Like arms on Timex,

Timeless,

Standing still as your toes align northward in pointed shoes,

Calloused,

Skin glowing with dedication,

And you make it,

Look so tasteful,

I've never seen a nutcracker so graceful,

In awe,

I am,

In shock, because the one person that's supposed to adore u,

Scorns ur talent like it's a death sentence,

Avoiding your sue-ten-oos like the bubonic plague,

As if he's going to catch ur gay, from plies, and leotards,

And it's hard,

Butch Queenin,

But you make it look easy,

My b-boy, black, bitch, boy ballerina,

Your tears stream fluidly as u leap, praying that you'll one day be good enough, strong enough, man enough to win his approval,

Against the beam u rest inhaling,

Toes pointed forward bracing for the inevitable,

My ballerina boy,

Defying every myth,

Shattering your glass ceiling u soar,

Over-extending,

Gender blending,

Beauty at the apex,

Perching gracefully on your throne,

A champion,

Proving once and for all,

That real men do wear tights.

Colors

Ryan's favorite color was red,

He used to sport those high top Chuck Taylors, speckled with amber highlights and ivory shoe strings, clean creased dickies with a crisp Hanes tee, fresh out the pack, standing tall and proud,

Pants sharper than the razor that etched 2 stripes on the cusp of his left brow, he stood, head higher than the top of a sycamore tree, validated by his status as an ace.

Ryan's favorite color was red, the same hue that marked the emotion shed from his heart, as the bullet pierced a pulmonary, permanently silencing him.

My cousin's favorite color was blue, radiating, intertwining with the ivory, he signed his name to the tablet, hoping to adorn a royal jacket with a crest and shield, only to be yielded by a brother's fist, the blow,

Was so swift it sent a cease message to his cerebral cortex, and shot his hopes into the threshold of eternal dreams.

In every city, there's a child, discouraged from the grind only to die over colors, these organizations, cock strong, glocks blazing, roll hard, go harder, 'til our father is spoken and the line is broken by another homicide, solidarity solidified in broken bones and bruised knuckles, cuz the whole block chuckles when jocks get the wood, and Ryan? His favorite color is a memory, my cousin's life is history, and piru alpha beta sigma theta is to blame for our misery.

For every "Becky", there's a Brenda,

13 year old, belly full of promise, feet swollen from walking the path trodden,

Hurt not by Bin Laden, but by her own people,

I heard a poet say once that black girls don't go crazy, and I agree,

Fuck, street, dumb and ghetto, in court they plead insanity, on my screen I can B-E-T on the images, selling poison in blue boxes, with white tops and red bows, gift tag signed: industry Pinocchio, and as their nose grows, we need no-doze to WAKE UP and see what's in front of us,

For every "Becky", there's a shawty got ass, baby got back, shawty got the clap, and I can B-E-T on ur MTV they don't talk about HIV or is it VH1?

Social Control is disguised as pop music, and as Americans "take the gun" staring down the barrel of destruction, they sign a pact in exchange for their minds and souls, polluted and di-luted by the imagery of constant repetition, now watch me "Yule" outta school and shake my ass into submission, and give it up one time for the Hottentot Venus, they say black girls don't go crazy, they're just lazy, till we tell 'em "shake dat ass bitch and let me see what you got" and I can B-E- T on ur MTV that's all you'll see, cuz for every "Becky" there's a shorty that's a nameless commodity, and we don't hear about those black girls bound by invisible straight-jackets writing in their diaries, scribbling out their frustrations, spines broken from the weight of all the "isms" coupled with commercialism and materialism, and all because we love you, we re-name you Chicken-heads and hoes, strip you of your clothes and sell your legacy to the highest bidder, neglecting to consider a 400 hundred plus history of rape and bondage, and "I ain't saying she a gold digger", naw the issue is way bigger and I can B-E-T your MTV ain't playing that song,

2pac spoke of Changes but no progression, and his lesson in "keep ya head up" was riddled by bullets, and the best Queens can get these days is a Diva, still a bitch but at least she's in control, in lingerie and heels screaming "booty-licious" and just cuz it's in the dictionary doesn't mean that it's permissible to say, to chocolate girls walking down the street,

Hip-Pop culture, is operating in the house that race and patriarchy built, ideology embedded in our consciousness, this poison, in our minds is infiltrating our lives, and even the most liberal among us have to de-program stereotypes before meeting a black girl in shorts and a tube top, trying not to focus on anatomy, and listen to her voice and "I ain't saying she a gold digger, naw cuz our issue is way bigger"

Life after College

Where I'm from

Blazing summers, barking dogs, sirens eclipsing creaking swings,

Where I'm from malls have curfews at 10'oclock only for chocolate kids in the city,

Teddy bears line street corners with liquor bottles and empty swings adorn abandoned playgrounds,

See,

Where I'm from classrooms are cold from lack of heat and bodies disappearing from the seats,

Have you ever had 3 friends die over glasses?

Cartier's make 'em crazy,

Where I'm from if you lazy, that deep breath may be your last,

Cops ain't gon help you cuz your just another nigga to the trigger,

And if you're lucky they'll come within an hour or so, the story goes,

I suppose I'm 'posed to be safe, with fiends jackin' and cops smashin' on Kreme's Krispy,

Tipsy,

Drunk off the blood sweat and tears of residents, testing the trust and integrity of the badge,

As years pass and other kids are slain from neglect,
and check from approval from the mayor,

Giving orders behind bars of iron, while dope-bois spit
bars of fire, dyin' to make it out the jungle,

Surviving as the illest, as poverty tries to kill us,

And still it's a struggle to get kids to open books, cuz
its too hard to read and easy to do chemistry, Cuz
baking soda, H2O and heat yields currency, and trees
lead to instant gratification,

But taking the easy way out leads to bracelets of
stainless steel captivity,

Where I'm from its either get down or lay down, or
grow up and show up with too many of my people
pushin' back eyelids and pushin' up daisies, leaving
too many babies crying alone in the dark,

Where I'm from, it's a handful of prodigies that make
it,

Surviving off of hopes and dreams, and opportunities
to breathe easy, never looking back to the past,
staying focused, cuz its get down or lay down,

Where I'm from, new buildings and creations, are
cultivated through education,

Show up and grow up is a matter of life and death and
knowledge is the only tool that saves you from
destruction,

Where I'm from

22

22, broken hearted,

Life still uncharted,

U,

Came and saved me, at 21 still heroic at 22,

Glass slippers filled, princess charming, darling U, cast a spell enchanting me, granting me,

More than 3 wishes, genies in bottles couldn't top ur simply irresistible -ness,

Stress free, except for real life, bachelor's degree, with honors no job, grad school in the fall,

Do I gotta work at McDonalds? Stress,

But I digress and expect you 2 be here with me, enduring,

Procuring our future, trips and memories, my b-day at 23 will be thankfully appreciated,

You've created, an impeccable fire within me, and no you ain't my dream girl,

We not takin' flights, we're sailing, over the walls we built,

And you don't wear a Halo, you have a set of wings, aerial,

Stunting over every hoe, really though,

I just thought you should know, you're my romantic getaway,

My weekend excursion, my single red rose, the Oreos in my ice cream,

The only 1 that can get me to drink rice dream,

U are the lady who has my heart,

And from my word I will never part, I love u in a place where there's no time or space,

And I thank God every morning I wake up to your face, breathing u, holding tightly, wishing it would never end, at 22 I have a partner whose also my best friend.

Amerikkka

America,

Amerikkka,

I used to sing your praises every morning,

My country 'tis of thee,

Now I refuse to stand up and sing Sweet land of liberty,

Liberty a figurative virtue in this land of bittersweet faculties,

Amerikkka,

I can no longer exalt you, of course no one can hold you higher than your own esteem

But as YOU proclaim "land of the free",

It's time that you should come clean

America,

You were the same one responsible for the systemic degradation of my people,

Bred from the KKK, Kill-her, Kill-him, Kill-'em Ideology, you single handedly made it possible for hundreds of thousands to be slain, Emmitt Till was a product of this game,

And a direct order was sent to Alabama making 4 little girls a warning to blacks in America,

But ever since the Birth of a Nation, there's been deliberation about the origin of black,

Nigger in fact, was a direct result of negative connotation,

America,

Made my ancestors inferior based on fear of superior qualities,

And obviously this mindset exists currently,

"Nigger" drop the "er" and add an "a" for American "Nigga"

How do you reclaim a name that wasn't given but assigned?

Intertwined with racism and white supremacy,

Paternalist practices ensued in the name of manifest destiny,

Forcing beliefs and a false image of God,

Pushing inferiority on those who remained in touch with tribal ties,

America the" Beautiful" founded on the strength of lies,

Breathing off the sweat of men,

Surviving on the blood of wives,

"Nigga" launch the "A" back to America Drop all the consonants,

Keep the "I" for Intelligent

Cuz the "A" is reassurance to keep all the niggas ignorant,

America,

Have you not a hobby?

Who else is in the business of destroying lives and legacies?

For their best interest,

America,

Where U.S stands not for "us" but U Surrender,

All your liberties, 'tis of thee into figurative identity American,

Arrogant, Materialistic, Executing, Rude, Ignorant, Condescending, Apathetic, Narcissistic Nation,

Creating everlasting frustration,

Among those whose education is still inferior to those in other locations,

America,

The only place where a fuck-up gets lost and gets his own holiday,

America,

Sweet land of liberty where the rich get richer to buy bigger butts to shit on the poor,

America,

The only place in the world that would sabotage their black leader and blame manufactured, actual, and natural disasters on him,

America,

I used to sing your praises every morning,

Now I refuse to stand up and sing,

Idolizing a land with slavery and homicide embedded in its constitution,

Hypocrisy between the lines of the bill of rights,

White,

Total Sovereignty and happiness,

Only can be attained,

In

Amerikkka.

Reflection

I am shadow,

Defined by rigidness as I check demographically,

The box non-Hispanic,

I am not a fucking swatch or a crayon, but my image is powerful,

Invoking the stealth of a panther,

Brazen ebony,

Hues radiate brighter than solstice sunlight,

I am Aphrodite, goddess of love,

My warmth spans globally, permeating the hatred bestowed upon me,

And he never asked me what I wanted, as he soiled my roots and nourished his branches, New rings appeared on my trunk, no longer pure of mother Africa tainted by Aryan blood, Yet I forgave him, trotting closer to the promised land behind my one and only,

Cross attached to his back while the noose hung loosely around my neck,

And I,

Re-incarnated as Athena goddess of war,

Wishing a motherfucker would test my strength, I embody creation,

Belly swollen with life, I breathe hope into despair,

Motivated against the wind as we marched on in Selma,

I imbrued miracles and sparked intelligence, as my breasts sagged with scrutiny,

Hips swayed with sorrow I became the Venus,

The fire between legs of lust,

Inciting unspoken pangs of hunger for my temple and thirst for my juices,

A vigilante I,

Took back the night and gave a "FUCK YOU" to conventional femininity,

And bit conservatives in the ass with my brash disposition,

Upright standing no longer bending over for doggy-style submission,

FUCK ME my way,

I'm tired of tradition,

I am SHE,

The improvement to the original, oozing with perfection, I am success, beauty, and order.

I am everything,

And NOTHING is possible,

Without

Me.

("My thoughts Inspired" Freestyle: Ottawa #2)

In November 2008,

They said segregation, racism was over,

But in Grand Rapids Michigan,

If you follow the red brick road,

There's a reason why the street is called Wealthy,

Bush ain't give a damn about a nigga, Negro, colored folk,

Still talkin' change and revolution,

Changes negated by the change in the pockets of senators,

Currency changing hands and still nothing changes but the weather, And whether or not you see it the youth is affected,

Protected by the culture of pollution called "nigga shit"

"They be like pause,

Dance, monkey dance,

You don't need a chance in my world, you'll just fuck it up,

Gave you a president, but it ain't enough,

Ur unhappy, you want a revolution,

We thought affirmative action was a good solution,

And u niggers still crying for some restitution,

Look at their chains, yeah they blingin ' ya 'll,

Poppin champagne, they still singin' ya 'll,

Poor healthcare, mediocre education,

Killing themselves for everybody's entertainment,

Dance monkey dance, go ahead and chew that bubblegum,

Don't open up those books cuz that's how we're gonna keep you dumb"

For all the blood that was shed on these grounds our,

Generations have lost sight of the mission, and recollection of fruition,

That eyes on the prize, listen,

Popped eyes and popped eyeballs, popped that casing of 380's,

Pop that coochie if you hear me cuz I'll teach you how to dougie,

But I can't teach you,

Open your eyes and stop poppin' those gats and poppin' those gums,

Read a fuckin book or you'll forever be dumb,

Now Imma teach you how to multiply, teach you how to read, teach you how to count a million dollars and some dreams, the only way to counter them is if you just believe, in the power of the pen and stop smoking on them leaves, shootin' up the silicone, and breakin' in Grand Prixs,

In 2008 they said racism was over but they only meant overtly,

No crosses are burning but the damage is subliminal,

Criminal actions and stereotypes implanted,

Of disadvantaged liberals,

Doomed by genetics and pigmentation,

Our youth generation has blinders,

Aimlessly billowing down a path to destruction,

Scholarship is more than an 11 letter free money equivalent,

So excuse me if I'm belligerent in my boycott of "nigga shit"

But I'd prefer to read and spend my time on things of value,

Gaining knowledge so I can curate Black culture,

Becoming a relic of royalty,

Saving people from extinction,

Developing resurgence,

In a positive direction,

Inciting a resurrection of Ebony Distinction.

I Used II Love U

I coulda married you,

We were engaged, not talkin' wedding bands around the third finger,

I mean,

I was entrapped by your spirit,

Your intellect engulfed me.

Cruel how could you,

Be so,

Iggin' me like Chico,

We were supposed to be Ashford and Simpson,

Besos like George and Lopez,

And though it's been awhile since you called,

My phone ain't stopped ringing,

Playing that same damn song and

I re-fuse to, be-lieve, you do, not think of me

As you're reading, tweeting, or driving, me, crazy,

With these maybe's,

And I don't understand the inconsistencies when

sincere-really you label me as the Judas,

As you impersonate the God, wearing your Halo as you paint me as a heathen,

But let me be the first to tell you,

That your shine is dingy, and no I don't need your prayers,

I say thine own, And Imma holla at the Creator who keeps a record of transgressions,

And progressive we can be to say "to hell with that" cuz all this shit is wack like,

The love poems you write or even the way you forsake me yet I betrayed thee?

And we all have our cross to bear so, tell me Mr. Perfect,

What makes you any different? You wanna cast the first stone amidst your own boulders,

And all this time I had your back, shoulders, knees and toes,

And hoes talk mad shit and you let em' but you say I'm the one whose loyalty I'm forgettin?

While this union we created you're the one who's neglectin',

But see,

This ain't no Taylor Swift album, and no I probably

won't make millions with 808's but this is my heartbreak,

Tears causing infernos, burning up my pillowcases,

Erasing all traces of your memories, in my mind,

And with time maybe just maybe,

I'll forgive you,

One day.

Happy Hour (Co-written by B. Tay)

B: I met you when I was 17,

A feeling that took me to monumental heights sight unseen

U were the alternate to my reality, U were the warmth in my midsummer nights' dream. It was you who I thought could never hurt me U were my escape from the pain of the world

It was U who could numb me...blur my vision...and make me feel quite lovely

K: At 13 my indoctrination with liquid courage was exhilarating,

Titillating,

Mocha complexion causing an erection and my marbles and nether region felt the perplexing artistry of my alternate reality,

Dancing like a gypsy in a Disney movie she,

Opened up and poured herself in a glass shaped like a timpani,

Like a,

Symphony orchestra player,

She had me slurring melodies and throwing back Bayer,

Head banger thumping,

Techno beat bumping,

She had me on the floor cry babying and humping

B: Your liquid courage is what kept my heart pumping

For 4 years you statutorily raped me

Still I found a way to love you

I wanted you to take me to long islands with plenty of sex on the beach

Taking flights with liquid marijuana's

And landing smoothly on clouds of Jose' and shots of 18,

Bottles of Patron made me feel so sexy

When I was broke, Smirnoff spoke to me and I felt like a new woman when I inhaled that Remy

I could never afford Moet but something about your top shelf body intoxicated me 'til I was nauseated, Sick to my stomach, with my head in the bathroom sink,

But still that wasn't enough to stop me

K: At 21, memories short like Napoleon, 151 embedded in senses, senseless thoughts coinciding with my actions, actin' like this night is never ending, everlasting, high ain't chocolate, but a rice grain 100 proof fallacy, dice games crapping me out, snake eyes glaring at me in the form of two shots, hypnotizing my psyche

one more round bartender,

Bring me those,

Buttery nipples, those red-headed sluts, blowjobs, and please no Shirley temples,

I been workin' too hard stressed out I need some comfort, down south with lime and coke that's what I come for

B: A banging headache wasn't enough to keep me away

It was something about your 100 proof that begged me to stay

That pinnacle had me so whipped and...

K: Kamikazes getting weaker and my tolerance is mighty, need some absinthe and a sugar cube to get my future right see, now my vision is obscured and my confidence is tight, bet you I can take her home by the end of the night, so I'm 'bout to hit this blunt book with Spirit and fly, I mean I'm 'bout to seal this deal at the end of the flight, and got no one else to thank but this, Crown Royal on ice,

Crown Royal on ice, Crown Royal on ice,

Crown Royal is...

Nice

B: Gallon after gallon I began to abuse you

K: Day in and day out I used and misused you

B: To drown out the voices

K: To numb all of my senses

B: We were like Batman & Robin

K: Now it's like Ike & Tina

B: Rollin down the river

K: Black eyes and bruised

B: Thought I was in control

K: Turns out I was the one being used.

I know you don't miss me, though we were together like cube steak and brisk teas,

Crisp cool, refreshing like the first dip in the pool you promised to teach me how to swim in,

Linen scented like the gain I inhaled from your sheets, sleepless nights were aplenty yet you were my comfort, not the kind I found in Mary, but soothing like the buttery velvet tone of Jill, as she, swooned over the melodies of saxophones and piano keys. I felt safe with you. Embraced with you, my fears and dumped all my sorrows in your recycling bin, and even then I never imagined that you'd be drifting on a memory, joy and pain was our melody but the sunshine and rain always handled it, whether good or bad, happy or sad we made a pact like Al Green, but something happened along the way so we couldn't stay together, got a fistful of tears, can't believe that you're far away, but stories end as a stories do, reality steps in but I can't get over you.

Pecola's Lyric

Black and blue,

Not colors of the rainbow but my rainbow love is,

Black,

Her heart a manifestation of insecurities,

It doesn't take Pecola to Breedlove but even she wanted eyes,

Blue

Like rhapsodies cuz lady sings the,

Blues like any other,

Deep like the ocean,

Black veins ashen,

Charcoal coating breaking broken,

Silence,

Shattering sonic booms of lonely vibrations,

Black roses wilting petals black,

Eyes and blue bruises

And no one ever chooses to be heartless,

She never asked to be a shadow,

Black,

A shell of cold emotion, no capacity to feel,

But a cesspool of feelings blue,

Lady sings the,

Pills fill her esophagus,

Blue face from lack of oxygen,

Black,

Her heart a manifestation of insecurities but surely we all knew she was beautiful, Always knew the right words to say,

Why did she,

Have to go,

Black,

To the point that she won't come back,

And her name wasn't Amy but she always kept a Winehouse,

To wash down the blue,

But she was a good person and all she needed was a shoulder to Breedlove but no blue eyes ever came,

Her mirrors played cruel games

And if only she could see that she was beautiful,

Her heart,

Would boom like an 808, kick like the amps in a '64 Chevy

Blues is what I sing now,

No rainbow heart,

Just a love I didn't choose,

She's gone now and left me nothing but this bruise

Your favorite color is purple, deep and royal, like the reign of your ancestors, you never knew, I wonder if you look in the mirror and see my reflection, cuz I see you in mine and you ain't mine but you look just like me, ebony on ivory your eyes zebra striped see you never knew who you'd become or where you're going, but I'm hopin the wind is blowin' in my direction, your reflection is beauty, and Imma beast like Disney, you could come into my castle love is waiting on the floor, hate is beating down my door listen...

I just want your rock so we can make a republic, that rock that make my heart quick, not the white but maybe colorless so when the sun shines it sparkles like stars in the moonlight, and if loving you is wrong,

then I'm still gon' write, every day for a year on some notebook 'ish, 'til my notebooks bent, papers loose and shit, 'til my words over flowin' broken levies and this, right I have to love freely, I do it finally, but fuck being famous, I just wanna claim a place this, beautiful for us to dwell, too much heaven to go to hell, in this fight we can prevail, because some people call us "homo", yeah we same sexin' but the sex ain't the same when I'm with you, to kiss you is to bottle up a thousand smiles and for your loving heart, I'd walk on glass for a thousand miles, yet time and space is you and I in other places away from one another, brokenhearted, keeping feelings undercover, lover, I been patiently waiting, for you I'd die trying, but this ain't materialized so for now I'm fantasizing.

HOMOCIDE

In our world walking outside is like combat,

Not Iraq but we live in terror,

Fatigues, boots, tied double knotted,

Trying not to trip on the duality,

Of being accepted and unacceptable in our society,

I think we need to declare the country in a state of emergency,

3 days ago a young boy died,

He wasn't killed or buried alive,

He committed suicide at 14,

Cuz being dead in a coffin was better off than being incarcerated in reality,

A young girl slices her wrist horizontally from end to end,

Wishing that her torture would end,

And she never wanted to be a memory all she wanted was to go prom with her lover,

Sick and tired of living undercover,

She,

Came out to her parents,

And apparently it was an abomination,

So she cuts to help ease her frustration,

A young boy,

Had dreams of going to college,

Wanted to be an engineer and build roadways and structures,

But fags can't be engineers or good roommates,

And when the sex tape surfaced he soon suffered an ill fate,

The rope snapped from the ceiling and he too became a cold case Listen,

People's lives are at stake,

Every day is a battleground with live mines waiting to explode,

And all we want is some armor to protect us from discrimination,

And maybe I should title this "To whom it may Concern",

So people who actually give a damn will read it,

We risk our lives daily for just breathing,

They give Ak47's and grenades to those who label us as heathens,

Little Larry was shot in class at 15,

And I think we need to start a revolution like Martin King,

Or start a March on D.C to the West Wing and,

Propose a house bill to eliminate bullying and make our families visual, Cuz the state of the nation's heart is in critical,

Conditions are fucked so do away with traditions,

Stop blaming your religion,

The gays you're killing are also Christians,

In our world walking outside is like combat,

Not the War in Iraq but a legislative attack,

But we'll keep fighting 'til we change our reality,

To being expected and accepted in our society.

I'm an entrepreneur, not talkin' business, my investment is social, capital is political and physically I'm a ticking time bomb, blocks of C4 line mind bombs lyrically my pad is a mine field with strategically placed phrases, blazin', burning, singeing features off people's faces, facing issues that's over dope, like how my colleague is a college grad ex-prostitute that's over broke, she's a grandparent, educated ex-felon that got over Dope, restored by her faith and belief in the American Dream, but that's only attainable if you play for the same team as those who are elevated by paper that's worth less than the sweat on your face, and it's a disgrace when young people get shot in schools and blown up at races, yet the media finds a way to remind us that we're still racist, went from "no suspects" to an ABP on a dark skin male with a backpack, and you can pack black skin in cargo ships and sail onward but any talk about race in America will forever be AWKWARD, cuz Manifest Destiny, slavery, and hate crimes will never hit harder than a bomb at a Marathon, gas stations bombing cars with bad "gasolina", and my daddy wasn't a Yankee, he was from Dominicana, red, white, and blue, didn't bleed blue blood, never had a silver spoon, or different strokes his facts of life were his pedigree, brown skin male in America his presence is noted critically, and critically I proclaim my status socially as a cynic, how my President is Black but Congress is shutting down clinics, students are dying while pledging allegiance to a flag that waves half-mast as rifles blast to signal open season, Olympus is falling with NRA cards maxing out like Visas, I think we need to revise our plan, put all the hatred in Pandora's Box and lock it, Let's start with addressing poverty, homeless kids and the decline of our moral compass, we can't re-write our history as a country if we don't know where we're going, but we know where we've been and the cycle keeps on going, we're destroying the ozone layer and blaming tsunamis on global warming, scapegoating mental health for mass murders when the papacies murdered the masses in Salem, I'm talking 'bout MLK in Memphis, Harvey Milk in California, and Sakia Gunn in New York, and my daddy wasn't a Yankee but Liberty is supposed to be free, but everything has a price, How much will you be?

An inhalant sends an immediate message to receptors that release serotonin in the body, giving way to a dopamine rush, a high that sends a feeling of joy to the mind, I wonder if I will feel like this on Sunday, but today as I drape the cap and gown over my shoulders, I give praise to who I believe is the owner of my life, whom I call the most high yet I cannot forget to acknowledge the ones who didn't make it, in admissions they call it retention,

I call it pay attention to detail, see my story is like one of many yet, I stand here today an owner, adorning a hood for which some centuries ago may have been used to demean me, and deny my personhood, a short time ago I was property, oppression akin to my people, ledgers full of flesh and bones, names and traits on rolls with bounties, barred access to different counties, now I stand before you crafting my own destiny because this moment is mine and I'm losing myself like Marshall Mathers, a young girl from 8 mile who found out that her voice matters, to populations in bondage within their psychosocial, and I refuse to believe that justice isn't social, so I decree that my degree is the deed to the house my ancestors built, as they laid the foundation, trudging blindly through non-violent social upheaval to the promised land, to reverse the reconstruction, and destruction of a malignant system of oppression, We hold these truths to be self-evident that all men are created equal, all men weren't regarded as people so how could they have all been equal? Toiling and working land that they didn't own, cultivating crops and raising children that were property of others, while being regarded as the other regardless of their, pulse, heartbeat, racing, rhythmic, in anticipation of a culminating moment, inhaling, taking the breath, before my first credit, I made the decision to own every first because second just isn't good enough, and I refuse to stay home like a Bronco, this is the Super Bowl, and I'm in rare form filling out all these forms like I'm owning, everything in my path, show me my limitations and I'll reverse the function, zero it out and show you that limits do not exist, my terminology is extensive, psychology existential, you don't have to be a rocket scientist to see that I got potential, and I refuse to waste it, I'll embrace it, no sitting there on the couch watching commercials, I'm cramming knowledge in a pint sized package making it commercial, like buildings downtown with bars from which I'm barred access, Excess is the law that drives this place, how my money is paying light bills and buying computers in new buildings with billionaire legacies, 5 families own everything in this town except MySpace, I hold that deed and made a profile so when they profile me, I don't fit the description, yet I'm conflicted because I promised myself I would carpe diem, every breath I take, Stings with the possibility of failure yet I succeed because I'm an owner of the titles Master of Social Work and Master of Public Administration, and as I'm inhaling, triggering the serotonin release, culminating in a dopamine rush, I am humbled, grateful to those who have sowed the crops and picked the strange fruits removing thorns from their calloused fingers, thankful that I will never be required to call anyone "Master" unless I'm looking at myself in a mirror.

For Burnie

A uniform, symbolizes professionalism and conformity, a standard attire that one must adhere to, but not you, in your pressed crisp whites, you broke barriers as one of few black registered nurses at the time, a time where black women were treated unequal, and people, would rather receive care from mirror images, you, in your crisp whites served those who didn't like you, your uniform a symbol of your heart as a servant, not talking Benson, Jeffrey on the Fresh Prince ain't have nothing on your loyalty to serve, cuz your talents weren't limited to your family they extended to all humanity, I remember my first call to service at your side, you asked me if I had any toys or stuffed animals to give away, my thoughts were selfish as I didn't want to give, but something about your spirit, your warmth allowed me to be unselfish, and when I saw the shelter that the toys would call home I knew that you were different, as a child I watched you give everything to the world, and want nothing, nothing in this world could compare to the times we spent, shopping and hiding purchases in every corner of the house, Grandpa never had a clue, how much retail we'd acquire, in your attire you would walk the track in pressed jeans cuz image was everything and you refused to get caught slipping, sliding money to me on the side with the promise not to tell Grandpa, after he'd already given me some, caring, never wanting anything in return you gave yourself to everyone, time, energy and even when there was nothing left you still always had something to give to the world, a scholar, you staying up handwriting papers on yellow legal pads to finish college, with cramped hands in the midnight hours, scribbling pages as mom was typing, fast forward to your graduation, the uniform was Kelly green robes and a mortar board cap and I knew that was a big deal, I knew that I wanted to be in your spot, walking across the stage with people cheering my name, perseverance, a nontraditional student, you finished, non-confirming, you taught me from an early age to be different, even though you said otherwise, your actions spoke volumes, and now, the silence is louder than a sonic boom, deafening, causing reactive attachment to your videos and pictures, I wear, my uniform in remembrance, my bowtie a symbol of service, colors symbolic of vibrancy, I picture, your uniform now, the crisp whites of nursing are replaced with new ones and a pair of wings, your legacy lives on through the people, I want your name added to the list of stars that ascend to the heavens, but really you deserve a lifetime achievement award for your contributions... I miss you so much already, way more than Whitney Houston, way more than Michael Jackson, no matter what Luther says a chair ain't a chair without you in it, but now you're a star, ever glowing, illuminating, shining brightly in the heavens, going on forever, and your loving light will never fade away.

Good Enough

She said you'll never be good enough,

And she was right,

You see she was used to,

All the other brothers,

Not immune to love and kindness,

Quite familiar with violence,

and liked to be best friends

With cheatin' and lyin',

So when I showed up she was really defiant,

Because,

I wasn't good enough,

Or maybe not bad enough or mad enough to slap her on her face and get tatted up,

But really,

I shattered all her myths about love and relationships,

And

As the ship kept sailing she kept flailing,

Gasping for air that she inhaled freely cuz I allowed

her to soar as her past kept holding her down,

She wanted me to hold her down,

like put money on her books but I was trying to put money on her books for classes,

Rehashing the same positive affirmations like "you're beautiful" "I think you're worth it"

And "nobody's perfect but you're perfect for me" but our ideas of love differed,

Like Different World V. Different Strokes,

I was in my books and she was taking ropes,

Tied to bedposts from Detroit to Chi-city,

All because I told her,

That I loved her,

That she was worth it,

And yeah "nobody's perfect but you're perfect for me"

But she said,

I'm sorry

You'll be never be good enough

And really she was right

I wasn't good enough,

I was too good...for her.

Shrink

Adichie once said "we teach girls to shrink themselves"

Young girls count calories,

While boys count bodies,

Tell me,

Is it fair to assume that our only purpose is to have no purpose other than procreation?

Twerking aimlessly as the body count rises,

Infant mortality rates increasing as young thighs attract,

We detract all the attention from this as the world watches,

People that represent no fabric of American reality portray our country as the land of gluttony,

Land of the free home of the brave,

Although it's still lethal for gays to be visibly married in most states,

With cowards who stand by and watch others get raped,

In public,

We turn blind eyes to wheelchairs and guys who fought in our wars,

With turned up noses, we look down on those who we deem unimportant unless of course someone says they are then we're all over them like whites on rice back in 1694, but of course in 2014, everyone is gluten free,

And something else is the new thing,

That we've stolen from someone else's culture and adapted as our own and destroyed it as only we do,

We emphasize our greatness,

Stretching our influence,

Of arrogance and ignorance tell me, what be the purpose of manifest destiny if not other than to manifest our ideas, commandeering cultures from other countries, like thieves in the day, we stole "gay" from the British, and everything else came from Native, Afro-Latino peoples

But we teach girls to count calories as boys expand,

And matter takes up space,

So tell me what am I supposed to say,

To my 16 year mentee who wants to be an engineer in a school with no robotics,

We emphasize our greatness yet our schools are below average, unless your per capita income is 6 figures,

I'll guess she'll figure out in these states of matter,

That she's Delaware,

and Johnny is Texas,

But in reality Johnny is flunking

He uses Adderall for football and cocaine on the weekends,

And she spends,

Hours studying in a home that she can't sleep in,

On the honor roll,

Yet she's regarded as a hoe,

Because her clothes don't fit,

So she's counting calories

Middle finger down her throat,

Trying to matter,

To Johnny,

And everyone else.

Leaving Pt. I

She said she's leaving,

I spent hours and minutes

And minutes and days

trying figure out what I'd say,

It's like a kamikaze jet plane exploded inside my pulmonary arteries,

Tell me,

How do I breathe without air?

She's silent,

Standing at attention,

About face,

Facing forward looking brightly at her future,

Her future,

At the same damn time,

I want our futures to align,

I ask her,

How long will you be?

She pauses,

Shrugs,

Athletic shoulder blades collapsing,

Lapsing judgments and bad decisions,

Looming,

Impending,

Doom, like the senses

I attempt to,

Catch my breath before I'm speaking,

I remember when I first saw her,

My brain was on shuffle,

Speech muffled I was nervous,

Palms sweaty in a daze, how could she be so beautiful,

Just yesterday we had an argument,

Now in the morning she's onward bound to Howard,

She said she's leaving,

And I say,

Go,

Follow your dreams

Pursue your heart,

Five heartbeats away from falling over,

Praying for sunshine but nights like this

Raindrops keep falling,

Tears burning up my pillowcases,

Inferno,

Ducts bursting like levies,

Drowning, engulfed by the floodgates

I see your face when you're not around me,

Presence haunting like the spirits we downed on our first date,

I can't hear it,

Can't bear the thought of losing the,

Bear hugs,

Bare rugs we pressed our grooves into,

Our fortress, perspires your Paris Hilton scent, pores filled with Vanilla fragrance,

Even for a little while the silence is daunting,

Deaf tones,

Zoned out spacing,

Folks in my face talking

Asking what does this mean?

Cuz she said she's leaving

And I say

Go

Cuz

Through my loneliness and uncertainties

I know the sum of my success and her accomplishments

Divided by the two of us means

A standard of life above average

She says she's leaving and I say...

"Heroine"

I could never be like her, that's what I always say, It's what I always think but I never actually had the courage to say these things to you, I mean, you look at her as though she's the one, as though she's the one that was put on this earth, for you, and I, always feel like the 6th man, see, you have her in your starting 5 your "fave" 5 or whatever you claim, whoever's carrying you these days but me, I'm the Boost Mobile to her T-Mobile and though she's terrible she's a larger carrier and I carry you when she holds you down and picks you up and puts you right back down, see, I could never be your heroine I've only tried to save you, but you're not addicted to me, and I'm not flowing through your veins, though your blood flows through mine, I'm only part of you, but not inside of you like she is, but you, love her honey complexion, sweet snow white Eskimo kisses, side chicks, act like main hoes these days, you can't afford to get some new tracks for your mistress, still this, chick is beside you, inside you, daily, and me, in the shadows, listening to Daley, where you left me, I could never be her, always wanted to be her cuz she has every part of you, she's got a hold on you so tightly, in a vice grip she, has you wrapped around her skin like a Chinese flytrap and I, in the shadows like always, you, crying desperately for me to save you, on the way down, but on a good day, you, flexing in your stingray, you, singing sweet sonnets to MJ like Rick James, you claim one day I'll be important, and one day you'll be mine again on the way down, and I'll always be down for you but your cycle brings me down more than 5 days a month, but I can only be your hero, but I alone can't save you, and no matter how hard I try I can never be your heroin.

Silent

Like a thief in the night, she snatched me

No grocery store prank in daylight, my twilights empty, sweet satisfaction, my craving for snack time is now hard to swallow, hollow, are my thoughts cuz I ought not be thinking of silent nights and holidays, kissing her tenderly under festive dressings, pressing my face into her essence, guessing her age trying to tell by the rings on her trunk, I ought not, dare not, envision what our world would be if things were a lot more civil, simple like the rules for dating Jim's daughter, but this ain't for show, this ain't TV, and the dad ain't Jim but it's him who makes the rules in Her fortress, silent, tears fall like lemon drops, sour, leaving a taste oral, my fixation with her oral skills is insane and we ain't even, touched the dream, but I believe in a dream deferred, but I'm deterred by her alarm that beeps like a guardian, silent, like the red light in the dash of my accord, I guess I'll record and play back all the almost moments, when she was happy right then, and I saw her light glistening, shimmering, shining like sun rays of potential, energy kinetic when ignited by my flame, vibrant, I know she got a lil' life in her yet she's tangled up in the towers of her fortress, want to call her baby, neo, take the blue pill and get caught up in her matrix, but this silence is forbidden, bitten, by the taste of temptation, more than contented by the touch of her purple kisses on my neck, I sigh and lent her my shoulder to cry onto, while fighting back my own, self-defense enacted, my plan of attack is to be the one that keeps her up at night, with my invisibility cloak I'll creep into her consciousness and wrap her up in my love, no she ain't Roni but my heart will belong to her, call to her, in the middle of the night, when peace is still, my piece will still bear the sweet of her lips and the scent of her, silently I call her name, as I gaze into her eyes, tears falling while she's staring at me, hearts in sync, I want to tell her all the things I've never said, a million ways that she is, but she is and I am...(silent)

"Sun"

Courageous, Fearless, unwavering...

These are words used to describe the essence of she, I always wonder if I can live up to the expectation of these weighty adjectives, heavy, bearing on shoulders like a party size bag of Doritos, the chips fall where they may and lately around here it feels like the 1800's in May, and, I refuse to stay silent but I'm haunted, daunted by the very purpose of my being as a creative, yet can stand before you and perform the craft "light as feather stiff as a board", binding, casting spells with descriptives, encrypted with entendres, I praise the most high for my gift but I won't bear one, you see, the thing that scares me most about creating is spawning greatness from my womb to the world only to have them broken, hoping that just one night the forecast will be mostly sunny with a chance of peace, but more often than not it's partly cloudy with a chance of pieces, streets are flooding with thc blood of the slaughter, daughters become only children, while we witness the re-birth of a nation, where white sheets are camouflaged with badges and blues, how can I feel safe in the world when my enemies are reds and blues? Blue jeans and hoodies soaked in struggle, Snuggle, still fresh from Purex washings, cuz days ago we celebrated his accomplishments, I even wrote a special message in his year book, it took, 3 seconds for all that to expire, all because my recipe required milk, 2 seconds playing cops and robbers, shooting the bad guys with dreams of being a hero, my fear about being creative is that I'll have to be courageous, fearless, and unwavering with cameras flashing, rehashing his potential for greatness, my creation, on social media pages, he had the prettiest smile was the best son ever, my creation, he had a scholarship to college and volunteered at non-profits, my creation, name spray painted RIP, in 2016 my fear of being creative is procreating and having a Sun, be eclipsed by evil and hatred, hate this time that we're living in, time wasted potential energy no longer kinetic, it's life less, my legacy will not be reduced to a fruit of the loom memorial but even I can't control my, type A wants to hold him close to me, shield him, pick up the pieces when he's shattered, broken, use crazy glue to reassemble his perception of red and blue cuz red and blue mixed together makes purple, royal, regal, his blood line is filled with legacies, and, his legacy will deserved to be remembered the way he crafts it, I can't, bear the thought of losing him, can't stand the sight of seeing the casket lowered six feet under ground zero, is where my heart lay, ground zero is where his heart stayed, I can't memorialize 9/11 if my heart needs 9-1-1 in Missouri, New York, Florida, Baltimore or Cleveland, his Arizona iced tea is spoiled, hoodie soiled from the blood of the chattel slaughter, my fear of being a creative and procreating is having a son, that could become a memory before his legacy is done.

In his life, 4 is a symbolic number, not some Jay-Z, Beyoncé fantasy, 4 is symbolic of bondage, bound to the normalcy of four walls, four bodies that he needs permission from to use the bathroom and 44 times he's moved from place to place, you see, this place is just like the others and his path mirrors the others but until you see the 16 anti-depressants and mood stabilizers on his medical record they'll tell you he's a bad seed. A plant that begins as a seed in fertile soil will grow, budding, sprouting, bearing fruits of a toiled journey I wonder in the cycle of life, if the plant enjoys the air it receives, majestic, the ability to turn carbon dioxide to oxygen, sun kisses and cool breezes in the wind, the only kisses he receives are those through the phone in his dreams, his nightmares far outweigh the REM cycle, his cycle of violence continued through his primary circle and landed him in number 44, he says in 5 years he's been to 44 placements and still there isn't a place meant just for him, where sleeping with the door open is a comfort and not a necessity, his seed was deprived of the tools necessary to survive, and as a defense he thrived off chaos, eliminating everything in his path, steam rolling, cuz being a man means more than showing emotion, and the only thing he knows is silence, for 4 years showing emotion meant bruises and scar tissue, tissues soaked from the silent tears of his uncle's routine, he sleeps with the door open as a defense, because closing it was an invitation, a violation of his privacy, he sleeps peacefully now, in these four walls, in number 45, I wonder how we can nourish his roots and restore his foundation, turn his concrete slab into fertile soil, restore his air quality and infuse his sunlight with hope and love. I wonder...

We hold these truths to be self-evident as a people, extinction is not only parallel to a triceratops but rather brown boys with high top fades and sneakers, speakers blare loudly as we nuance the necessity of what we pay attention to, assigning importance to respectable identities, intrinsically identifying to the powers that be, because we too sing America so much so that recognizing the suppression and silence of black women's beings and multiple identities is only good enough when white gaze is upon us, the last days are upon us my Grandma said but Grandma's dead and in spite of cancer, heart disease and HIV there's another thing killing us, homicidal, locked and loaded a red dot fixated on our foreheads, black men, black children, black women are under assault, pole vaulting over the bar of Olympic respectability politics is underway in a day and time where the President is black and the attacks on blacks are still prevalent, to date hundreds of known citizens have been murdered by law enforcement, enforcing white supremacy, causing us to assert that black lives matter at the same time questioning do they? Do they, have any idea how many miles it takes to understand the basics of being black in America, same gender loving non-conforming, educated, unduplicated, literally no one on earth has my name or spelling, it would probably take a couple marathons a decathlon and 5k to even fathom and still we in different leagues, I once watched a privilege walk video on

Buzz-Feed and the participant in front still didn't get it. To illustrate everyone starts on the same line and moves to and fro, back and forth based on questions posed and I suppose that I'm supposed to feel sorry for white males on MTV that find it difficult to talk subjugation and harassment from police, wrongful deaths and slander in the media attributed to institutionalized, Hold Up...They can't name it because it's too real for them to realize the benefits, but it's not uncommon for us to think that the 11 o clock news story could be my son, my sister, my partner, my mother, it's so difficult to empathize with apathy when I'm able to speak the names of Jordan, Eric, Trayvon, Sandra, Kindra, Oscar, Tamir, Sakia, Charleston and the list is ongoing notwithstanding the stories we don't hear about, transwomen and men that have to compete with other black lives killed all too often to gain remembrance, deliverance is understanding your role and subjugation, this nation built of the backs of others, "others" the creators, hunter gatherers' and cultivators that were concentrated, not in camps but reservations, and you wonder why I won't stand for the Pledge of Allegiance, when I can unlawfully die for just breathing and my people are continuously beaten, physically, psychologically, structurally in the streets and this ain't no call to your conscience, it's a, stream of consciousness, unconscious thoughts of how I'm feeling, reeling from this pain in dealing with, weight I'm carrying, burying, but I'm still praying, for change, for a brighter day, she was 28, an activist, natural hair and educated, sharp and knew her rights, promising future, beat the types of stereos, supersonic, Panasonic personality, voice in high definition, definitive of a strong black woman, no meek mills, I guess cops aren't equipped to deal with body builder types, I have the same prototype, subjected to the same archetype, typical of VH1 celebrities, it's no coincidence that victim blaming ensues for non-compliance, when presented in black female bodies, body parties are permitted without an invitation and any opposition is frowned upon as indignation, insubordination to the place the we're supposed to hold, the violence depicted, the silence inflicted tries to overshadow the rising sun, the phoenix, we are, making strides in every industry, the most educated minority, underpaid and unappreciated and this ain't no poem or allegory, this is a stream of consciousness, unconsciously unpacking my feelings, they say blacks don't run, my pain, my grievances, I'm running a half marathon, airing my emotions, emotionally because I deserve it, and contrary to what they think Black Lives Matter and Black Girls Rock and one day, one day, one day, these statements will end without a question mark.

Unnatural Causes Pt. I

We

We live

We live in a world where

there is no remorse

Just

recourse and discourse for our actions

and actions of others

othering their experience

experiencing post traumatic

cortisol releases

pieces

of my health and wellness

may as well just fade

Well less

often than those making

$250K

may well be

Well more

than those making $13

counting the number of pills it takes to

wake up and make it

cuz let's face it

We

We live

We live in a world where

there is no remorse

Just

recourse and discourse for our actions

acting like our neighbors choose their disposition

position as "Have Nots" and "Have Less"

and still it's

somehow better than being a

"Have None"

Fun is often a fleeting moment

abstract

an alternate reality

cuz the reality is

We

We live

We live in a world where working for others

is valued higher than

actually living

and life is existential

We can't

Live without living

yet

pure air is scarce

and

clean water has a price

We have successfully commodified

Life

and the quality of

Living

We

We exist

because most of us

can't afford

to start.

Atlantic Ocean SOC

A great rapper once said "I remember when you was conflicted, misusing your influence; sometimes I did the same"...Conflict, it starts as a whisper, like a Twister it picks up in crescendo, indo, only good when consumed outdoors during the pouring rain, I guess when it rains it pours salt water, Frank Ocean sang about Oceans, not 11 or 12 but the tears from a child, she was 13 when she first saw her mother weeping, sauntered over an obituary her willow was truncated, fixated on the manila photo of her father, who art in heaven, but where are you now when she needs you? She pleaded for him to stay home when the they got his order wrong and forgot the pickles, laughing, playing tickle tummy 'til bedtime, he promised to return but never did, guess the notion that tomorrow's not promised, not guaranteed, to brown skin brothers is a looming thought, consuming every black and brown child in the U.S. but her daddy wasn't deviant, he was an allegiant, sworn to protect and serve his badge number was N-Y Crooked Number so and so, guess the protect and serve mantra only works for so and so and not Papi, she at 13 had to understand why the ocean tastes bitter, sweet memories of a life lost yet she lost it all breaking her silence, having knowledge doesn't guarantee being free from social bondage, hit in the face with reality with no one to scream "Vonage", she had to realize at an early age that salt water is bitter...sweet.

HAIKU #1

EVERFLOWING WATER

RUNS RAPIDLY THROUGH MY SOUL

SLOWLY I'M DROWNING

The instrument God has blessed me with is the very thing that many die playing, It's not coincidental that the first book I read about empowerment was "Speak", the first political movie was "Raise Your Voice", the first song learned in chorus was "Lift Every Voice", I remember being conflicted, No Kendrick, No Cole in my stocking, I was a good girl, memorized all the Presidents with one day having hopes of being among the ranks, not Shabba but you don't understand me, Juvenile is how you see me but I'm changing the trajectory of a female, black and disadvantaged, 3 strikes not in California but in life, implanted in a hostile place, seeing people with screwed up faces when I enter the room, thinking "who are you", it must be nice that, whites don't have to go through this, "why are you here?" they ask, well now, I'm here so I can stake my claim, not an anomaly, I'm probably, an extraordinary but contrary case of intellect, emotional intelligence, effervescent, not meant for anything less than existing on the throne of excellence.

Fox say

Opioid use is a huge epidemic but demonized addiction in the "War on Drugs" that took our fathers and sons,

Suns set and moons rise,

Yet somehow “Moonlight” don't get shine,

Fox say

We need law and order forgetting that

The laws ordered the steps of our current condition,

Conditionally regarded,

Only as a political tool for 3/5ths

Of weapons of mass destruction

In communities,

Fox say

The decline of the moral compass has led to,

The decline of the nuclear family,

All while,

Nuclear families are obliterated

By tomahawks and tough talk on crime

Fox say black women are often angry,

Neglecting to consider,

The generations impacted by seeds of alternative facts

Fox say,

Exactly what it needs to

Say nothing

That hasn't already

Been broadcasted by men in white sheets

Women in "Pussyhats"

Or

Government talking heads

Heading up a system

Systemically designed for our demise

Prized possessions

Turned people

People act like

This is a new era

Fitted 8 years

Of homeostasis

On top of a structure that's racist

Placed this,

Fallacy of an alternate reality

In our faces

And now

Fox say

Everything it needs

To keep you.

Endangered Species

I am strong,

I am loud,

I am woman,

I am proud,

I'm a fighter,

I'm a lover,

I'm a daughter,

I'm a sister,

I cheer and I lead,

Try to erase me,

You won't succeed,

I build bridges,

Foundation laid,

Don't take for granted,

The road I paved,

The toll I paid,

For this light,

I am day,

I am night,

I am woman,

I ignite,

I am black,

Civil right,

I am Muslim,

I'm Latino,

I am Arab,

Filipino,

I'm an immigrant,

I'm American,

I'm a resident,

I'm a citizen,

My life matters you hear that part,

Black lives matter you hear that part,

I am human,

My life's endangered,

But you won't help me,

Cuz I'm a stranger.

To exist or not to exist, that is the question?

well Merriam Webster tells us that existing means quite simply to be, so if existing is to be then pre-existing would mean to be before, we were before, my government tells me that everything about me is a pre-existing condition, conditionally meant to oppress me into this category of "have-not" or disenfranchisement, not being able to fully participate in the rights therein or even be regarded as a human, right? So general condition of women, to be raped, to be pregnant, to be a procreator, the general condition of being black is to be at risk and to be a woman is to not be regarded or protected, so tell me if we were the first of mankind how is it that my pre-existence is a condition that is used against me? My country tis of thee, my country tis of thee does not want me here, but here in this city, we have the opportunity to Be, to exist, pre-reconstruction, pre-revolution, shaping the evolution of these hope zones, zoning out, forward marching, grassroots feet racing, pacing for a Riverbank, running full steam, dreaming of the day when unity doesn't cost, the price of innocence, night terrors,

And shots fired from shiny blues and scuffed shoes,

It starts as a whisper,

A ripple,

causing confusion, waves, disrupting the American way, status quo, no, woe is me ideology, typologies, I turned on the TV and saw nothing, the revolution will not be televised, the revolution will be tweeted, the revolution will be on IG, and snapped to your nearest LG, IPhone, Galaxy, smart phone, we don't have to record all the moments that humanity was at its lowest hoping that one day we can see each other as we see you and me like, blood, bones, eyes, ears, nose, mouth and teeth, teeth knocked against the pavement, waiting patiently for a leader to rise up against the chaos yet, sis said "we are the ones we've been waiting for" so let's stop waiting, making the case to sit by blindly idly waiting for someone to take the reins and rein in all the stuff that we've been going through, sowing through, seeds of promise, in our neighborhoods our children are watching, walking home from schools and playgrounds in social bondage, school to prison pipeline, keystone, poison, black gold, iron, veto, we go, crazy trying to make sense of all these pieces, Reese's had sense enough to combine peanut butter and chocolate yet we treat this, feat like an anomaly, collectively impacting our taste buds, we can convene to taste bud, light up, spark plugs, say "cuz", shed blood, roll up, now we have to show up, stronger, together, and no I won't co-opt a slogan from political actors, this ain't Hollywood, this is reality, no TV, and we can do more for the revolution than just tweet, or upload a status, cuz the status of our community is flat lining and we have the charge now to do more than pre-exist, we resist, we resist not just co-existing but existing with purpose, walking in light, collective, synergy, shining, bright like blood diamonds, we are the ones we've been waiting for, we are the ones we've been waiting for, we are the ones we've been waiting for, take your places.

Dear Mama

Dear mama,

You did your job so well

I can't possibly think of being your successor

A worthy predecessor you

Took care of everything

And nothing all at the same time

You did everything you could to make me

Everything I am

And for that I'm thankful

I thank you,

For all your countless sacrifices,

I thank you,

For all your sleepless nights

I thank you for everything

And nothing

You lost your one true love,

Your only son,

And gave up all your love to me

I could never repay you

I could never displace you

And though you feel like I'm accomplished

I could never outpace you

For you've given all you have to the world

So I say

To my dear mama

I love you

Even though the world mistreats you

And treats you

Like you're replaceable

No one

Can ever

Replace you.

Blood

Red

Like the color of cherry wine

my blood is fine

like the lines on my Grandmother's forehead.

Red

like the skin tone of my Grandfather

Cherokee blood borne,

no pathogens or pathological patterns but red like

the neck of a libertarian Aquarian waiting to make me leak red,

like the blood moon

it comes once in a while like my daddy,

popping up like a fresh pimple during that time of the month

when uterine walls drop red cells piece by piece,

slowly,

deteriorating

but generating new life

like John Redcorn in King of the Hill, but for a Black girl like me

the kings of these hills will always be painted

Red

like the contrast of November 2016 on the electoral map,

these streets bleed red and will only cease when "Redbones" awaken

but there's no need to wake up if you stay woke in the first place

and West Michigan is the first place where I feel nothing and everything at the same damn time

no future here for the redbones unless you're married

Cuz

Single ladies

only stay single for so long

and so long are the days when my walls bleed red mourning,

Creating a sacrificial lamb of your incubating space,

Heartbeat red at 22 weeks

guess I'll

have to catch the red eye to heaven to finally meet you,

greet you with red lips on your forehead lines

Defined

My blood born

Red

About the Author

Keyuana Rosemond is a multidimensional leader and poet from Metro Detroit. As an LGBT Black woman, she has a heart for service, equality, and expression. She earned MSW and MPA degrees from Grand Valley State University in 2010 and 2014 respectively, before beginning a career in Public Health and Nonprofit Administration. She serves diligently as a community advocate, constantly working to advance access to resources in urban areas in order to improve health conditions. She leads the Equity Drinks initiative in Grand Rapids, MI, and finds great joy in facilitating group strategy sessions and public speaking. In her spare time, Rosemond enjoys lifting weights, long runs, traveling, and eating good food with great people. She is a proud member of Sigma Gamma Rho Sorority, Incorporated.

Made in the USA
Lexington, KY
21 January 2018